T0114678

365 Love Quotes

Willie L. McClary

WESTBOW
PRESS®
A DIVISION OF THOMAS NELSON
& ZONDERVAN

WestBow Press books may be ordered through booksellers or by contacting:

WestBow Press
A Division of Thomas Nelson & Zondervan
1663 Liberty Drive
Bloomington, IN 47403
www.westbowpress.com
844-714-3454

ISBN: 978-1-6642-9633-6 (sc)
ISBN: 978-1-6642-9632-9 (e)

Print information available on the last page.

WestBow Press rev. date: 05/23/2023

Introduction

As Christians, love is not just what you say, it's what you do. What are you doing to show your spouse how much you love them? Marriage requires you giving your best at all times; 100 percent because in marriage we have to give in order to make it work. Love quotes are a great way to express how your feelings for the one you love.

Here are a few ideas on how to use these wonderful quotes for your spouse:

1. Write them on a post-it notes and leave them where they can be found.
2. Text them.
3. Send a quote to his or her e-mail.
4. Write them on a letter and send it to them via mail.
5. Write them on the bathroom mirror with lipstick or use candles with messages on each of them.
6. Say a love quote each day for a year.
7. Print it on a mug or cup for him or her.
8. Write a quote and put it on or in their Bible.

These deep romantic love quotes are sure to add a touch of romance to your relationship. Whether part of a Valentine's Day card, wedding vows, anniversary, or just an everyday way to say, I love you. You know your spouse or sweet heart would love receiving one of these romantic love quotes every day.

Communication and marital closeness make for giving better intimacy and definitely can bring back the romance in your relationship. One of the best ways I've found for maintaining closeness is by working through

a couple's devotional together. This awesome couples' devotionals go deep on important topics that matters to Christian couples. Everything from forgiveness to communication issues to better intimacy. I love that its goal is to help you create the healthy habit of better marriage communication in one year or less.

One of the best love quotes that captures marriage is by Mignon McLaughlin when he stated, "A successful marriage requires falling in love many times with the same person". In the kingdom of God, a strong and successful marriage is that person unconditional love and respect. It requires waking up every morning and be willing to give 100 percent of our attention, love and effort. Especially during hard times, because when we do; God takes our union to his Potter's wheel to mold, to bend, shape, and refine us into his holy image. And what a beautiful reflection we become! As you read these quotes it will strengthen your marriage and your relationships. As you read allow God to move in your hearts to show you what areas of your marriage or relationship need his strength, healing, and faith.

"A new commandment I give to you, that you love one another; By this all people will know that you are my disciples, if you have love for one another", (John 13:34-35 KJV). Having a Godly marriage shows the world that Christ's love through sacrificial love and service to one another. The same love that Jesus gave when he gave his life for us. Only leaning on a faithful father and longing to please him with everything that we do will set the stage for a beautiful romance. Marriage is not about staying together, but keeping a covenant. "Till death do us part", or "As long as we both shall live" is a sacred covenant promise-the kind Jesus made with his bride when he died for her. Men who sanctify his wife understands that this is his divinely ordained responsibility...Is my wife more like Christ because she's married to me? Or is she more like Christ in spite of me? Great marriages don't just happen by accident; they are the result of consistent investment of time, thoughtfulness, forgiveness, affection, prayer, mutual respect, and

Willie L. McClary

a rock-solid commitment between a husband and a wife. As husbands, we should be able to look our wives in the face and say, "You complete me". This is why the Apostle Paul says that to love your wife is to love yourself (Ephesians 5:28 KJV). The two are really one, and this means more than sentiment, it means they are one flesh.

To solve a marriage problem, you have to talk with each other about it. Take care to listen more than you speak. The lord blesses the couple with love and hope and keep alive the vows they've pledged. The Lord will bless their dreams and visions, and keep them safe, always.

"Love Must be sincere. Hate what is evil, cling to what is good", (Romans 12:9 NIV). I pray that by confessing your love to one another that your marriage will always bring glory to God, joy one to another and blessings to your families for many generations to come. May love and laughter fill your hearts and your homes for all the days of your lives. May you face every challenge knowing that with God's grace, you'll conquer all obstacles together. May the world be a better place because the two of you fell in love. The lord is the author, perfector, and the foundation of marriage. The world has twisted what marriage is intended to reflect, in a world that tries to tear at the very fabric of the union that the Lord has ordained. I pray that the God will keep our eyes open to the Satan's tactics, strategies, and distractions. Fight for your marriage by submitting one to another, and encouraging one another by having the same love one to another.

1. **To Her:** *Love takes off the masks that we fear we can't live up to. I will do my best to share this deep intimate love I have for you.*

   To Him: *We have true love, we weathered the storm, went through many tests and we are still here. Together forever; I love you.*

2. **To Her:** *You really have to love yourself, in order to love someone else. I love who I am becoming, and I promise to love you the same. Love you so much.*

   To Him: *You have found true love when you want to wake up to the same person every morning, even when you've have had differences. Love conquers all, love never fails.*

3. **To Her:** *I love you, that's the beginning and the end. No one else can compare to you. What we have is special.*

   To Him: *You mean everything to me. What we have is God given. You are my heart and my joy. Love you so much.*

4. **To Her:** *The most important thing in my life is to love. To give knowing that I will receive love in return. Good measure press down, shaken together and running over, shall you give me back in return (Matthew 6:33 KJV).*

   To Him: *You are nothing short of what I need in my life. Thank you for being my provider, comfort in storms, my man of God.*

5. **To Her:** *A man should never stop showing his wife how much she means to him even after he's got her.*

   To Him: *I thank you for the Priest that you are in our home covering us like only you can.*

6. **To Her:** *My ten-word love story: I can't imagine life without you. My love, My life.*

To Him: *What are the next thoughts after prayer before I drift to sleep and when I woke up the next morning? You are!*

7. **To Her:** *I love you not only for who you are, but for who I am when I am with you.*

To Him: *You are not a dream, you are my reality. I am blessed to have you by my side. Love you.*

8. **To Her:** *You are every reason, every hope, and every dream I had about marriage should be like with you.*

To Him: *Love is not about how many days, weeks, and months you've been together, it's about how much love we share each day.*

9. **To Her:** *I am a lot better person now then I was before I met you. You help make me what I am today.*

To Him: *I know what real love is, because of how you love me.*

10. **To Her:** *Sometimes love is spontaneous; a sudden inner impulse sometimes unplanned, unrehearsed action that makes your day everything it was purposed to be.*

To Him: *As I look into your beautiful eyes, I see a man of character, strength, wisdom and humility. I'll forever be yours.*

11. **To Her:** "I can't stop thinking about you, today, tomorrow, always."

To Him: This world is full of chaos and trouble, but there is one thing of which I am certain ;;my love for you."

12. **To Her:** Your touch, your hair, your smile really makes my day. I am so in love with you.

To Him: If I did anything right in my life it was when I gave my heart to you.

13. **To Her:** I am so totally, completely, over whelming, eye-popping, life changing, passionately in love with you.

To Him: The best and most beautiful things in this world cannot be seen or even heard, but must be felt with the heart.

14. **To Her:** I awake this morning and was reminded of the preciousness of life. I realize I should express my gratitude to you, because you are so important to me. Thank you for all you have done and have a great day.

To Him: Thank you for going on this journey of life with me. There is nobody else who I want by my side, love you.

15. **To Her:** Life without your love is like a tree without fruit, or flowers without blossoms, love you so much you.

To Him: What do I never get enough of? Your love. Together for the rest of our lives.

Willie L. McClary

16. **To Her:** *My favorite place to be is with you. When I say I love you, I'm reminding you that you are very special to me.*

To Him: *I'm indecisive about many things. But without a doubt, you are my favorite everything*

17. **To Her:** *You know you're in love when you don't want to fall asleep without my wife beside me.*

To Him: *To be your friend was all I wanted. To be your wife was all I ever dreamed of.*

18. **To Her:** *I couldn't always express how much you mean to me until now; I can say with a smile; "Whenever I'm with you, I feel complete. You are the love of my life".*

To Him: *I don't want to lose you in any way. I love the attention you give me. I love the way you make me feel*

19. **To Her:** *I am past the pride, anger, or any kind of emotion that would keep me from loving you.*

To Him: *Who would have thought that I would marry the most wonderful person I've ever known. Love you.*

20. **To Her:** *My heart is and always will be yours; Sexy lady.*

To Him: *My heart is filled with love design to embrace you forever. Every day with you is better than the day before, marriage is a pleasure with you.*

21. **To Her:** There can be no misunderstanding where love is shown. The love that I have for you helps me to understand you.

To Him: I want to be one of the reasons you smile, because surely you are one of the reasons I smile.

22. **To Her:** When I'm with you, you make me feel great. I love you. You are that one in a lifetime dream come true.

To Him: You make me feel safe in your arms, never let me go.

23. **To Her:** What makes my mornings even better is knowing that you will be mine forever. Love you so much.

To Him: I'll never give up on you, I'll never leave you. Instead, we will work through it together seeking guidance from the almighty God. A sure path of happiness.

24. **To Her:** I love your smile, your voice, your eyes, your body, and your laugh. I'm in love with you.

To Him: There are so many reasons I love you. Your handsome, intelligent and you have a great heart.

25. **To Her:** I am forever grateful for the joy and happiness you have brought into my life.

To Him: Loving you baby is a pure delight.

Willie L. McClary

26. **To Her:** *As I look into your eyes, I see a gift from God. Tailor made just for me, sweetheart I'm honored to have you in my life.*

To Him: *As we embrace each other, I love every stroke of your hands. You know me all too well. I want more of you.*

27. **To Her:** *Just when I thought that it was impossible to love you anymore more, you prove me wrong.*

To Him: *When I look into your beautiful brown eyes, you melt my heart. You mean so much to me.*

28. **To Her:** *Love is when your happiness means more to me than my own. I'm going to make you the happiest woman in the world.*

To Him: *The best feeling is being love by you. Being deeply loved by you.*

29. **To Her:** *Sometimes the two people who are truly best for each other are faced with great obstacles which brings them closer to each other.*

To Him: *Communication is vital in every marriage along with a strong prayer life which brings about great illumination; allowing your wisdom to be displayed.*

30. **To Her:** *Wow! What a beauty to behold this morning. Absolutely gorgeous.*

To Him: *Your love stirs my soul, your touch entices me, and your faith gives me strength. With you as my husband, I feel the love of God that gives me peace over all things.*

31. **To Her:** *We are to love each other without stopping to inquire whether or not the other is worthy. But what we are ask to do is love unconditionally.*

To Him: *Love is to keep forgiving each other's past mistakes. I want you to be more than just a moment I want you to be there for a lifetime.*

32. **To Her:** *When you came into my life, it was as if you had always lived there. My heart is a home built just for you.*

To Him: *I'm amazed when I look at you. Not because you're so handsome but because you are everything I've ever wanted.*

33. **To Her:** *You are amazing, you are completely different than anyone that I've met. It's like you took the best parts of yourself and hid them from the world and saved them just for me.*

To Him: *Power from within me comes from strength that also resides in you. Love is the most powerful force in the world. I love so very much.*

34. **To Her:** *The moment I met you we had an immediate connection. A connection so strong that I was drawn to you in a way I never experienced before. Overtime we have experienced a love so deep, strong, and complete that we could never be apart.*

To Him: *I love you more. I love you more than the bad days ahead of us, I love you more than the disagreements we've ever had. I love you more than any obstacles that could try to come between us. I love you the most.*

35. **To Her:** *A real marriage is two imperfect people refusing to give up on each other.*

To Him: *I don't want anyone else to have your heart, kiss your lips or be in your arms, because that's the only place I want to be.*

36. **To her:** *Once in a lifetime you meet someone that changes everything. You are that someone. I love you so much.*

To Him: *Great relationships doesn't just happen. They take time, patience, and two people who truly want to be together like us.*

37. **To Her:** *My favorite part of the day is when I get to talk to you. I love you because of how I feel when I'm with you.*

To Him: *My favorite place is inside your hugs and the feel of your lips kissing me over and over again. I promise there want be a day that I stop loving you.*

38. **To Her:** *Great marriages aren't great because they have no problems. They're great because two people care enough about each other and are determine to make it work.*

To Him: *I love you not because of anything you have but because of the love I feel when I'm with you. Simply amazing.*

39. **To Her:** *I know that I haven't been the best husband that I could be, but I promise to love you with all my heart.*

To Him: *I love when you rollover, and put your arms around me pull me close to you that makes me feel secure and complete.*

40. **To Her:** *You make me happy in a way no one else can. If I could turn the clock back, I'd fine you sooner and love you more.*

To Him: *I promise to support you in whatever you choose to do. I promise not to judge you. I promise to be honest with you. I promise to remind you every day how much I love you. I promise to never to break your heart, my only request is that you love me the same.*

41. **To Her:** *I have found the one whom my soul loves. (Song of Soloman 3:4 KJV).*

To Him: *When I'm with you I feel like I'm right where I belong. You mean everything to me.*

Willie L. McClary

42. **To Her:** *I feel happiness at the thought of loving you for the rest of my life.*

To Him: *I want us to have an amazing marriage. You're all I ever wanted in a husband.*

43. **To Her:** *If someone asked me, what I saw in you to love you so much my answer would be everything.*

To Him: *I'm completely in love with you. I think about you in the morning and before I fall asleep at night.*

44. **To Her:** *Before I met you, I never knew what it was like to be able to look at someone and smile for no reason. You bring out the best in me.*

To Him: *When you truly love someone, you will never let them go, no matter how difficult life is.*

45. **To Her:** *I love you with all my heart, my love, I can't get enough of loving you.*

To Him: *I can't get enough of your love, baby.*

46. **To Her:** *God has empowered me to love you as I should. What a pleasure to love someone like you, sweetheart.*

To Him: *I can't imagine my life without you. I love you.*

47. **To Her:** *I love you because you bring out the best in me.*

To Him: *You make me feel so confident. I cannot contain the love that I have for you.*

48. **To Her:** *I'm always thinking of you and the time we spend together. I'll marry you all over again if I had the choice. No regrets.*

To Him: *No matter how tough life gets, nothing is worse than being apart from you.*

49. **To her:** *Love is all I have; love is all I need. My love for you is always there.*

To Him: *I love you, always remember that you're all that I need.*

50. **To Her:** *The opportunity to love you is now. No matter what happen I always will.*

To Him: *I've never loved anyone in this world as much as I love you right now.*

51. **To Her:** *You are my favorite person to be with. I love you and nothing could ever change that.*

To Him: *Our relationship is not perfect, but the love we have for each other make up for all the small imperfections.*

52. **To Her:** I've never had a moment's doubt. I love you. I believe in you completely. You are a great woman, my love.

To Him: I love you, and that is all that matters. Nothing and nobody, not even time will change that.

53. **To Her:** Sweetheart you are dear to me. You are the reason why I express my love so much.

To Him: Whatever happens tomorrow or for the rest of our life, I'm happy because I have you. love you so much.

54. **To her:** Your beauty has my attention, but your personality has my heart.

To Him: I wish time could stop when I'm in your arms, because it's one of the best feeling I have when I'm alone with you.

55. **To her:** For all the things my hands have held, the best by far is you.

To Him: I love to feel your biceps as you hold me the way you do, my love.

56. **To her:** You're simply the best, so now it's clear that I need you here by my side, always.

To Him: My angel, my life, my entire world, you're the one that I want, the one that I need.

57. **To Her:** *Words cannot express how I feel about you. I love you because you understand me, you support me, and encourage me to reach my goals.*

To Him: *I value our relationship more than you will ever know. You are the man of my dreams; baby and I am definitely satisfied.*

58. **To Her:** *Sweetheart you are my masterpiece, what a beauty you are to behold.*

To Him: *You will always have a special place in my heart. You are the best, finest, courageous, encouraging, the most wonderful person that I have ever known.*

59. **To Her:** *May you excel in all you set your hands to my lady, my love. To him: You brighten my day, you make my heart beat faster. My love, my everything. The only one I need. I love you so much.*

60. **To Her:** *My love for you runs deep, the more I give to you, the more I have to give. My love for you is infinite.*

To Him: *You are my covering each and every day I appreciate you so much.*

61. **To Her:** *Every day that I'm with you means so much to me; filled with love and laughter.*

To Him: *When I look into your eyes, I see a mighty man of valor. Full of strength and vigor.*

62. **To Her:** *I have waited so long for the perfect woman, and my patience finally paid off when I met you.*

To Him: *I can't stop thinking about you yesterday, today, tomorrow and forever.*

63. **To Her:** *I may not be perfect, but I have truly found the perfect woman for me. You saw something in me that somehow gave me direction again.*

To Him: *I know that I've found my true love, because my reality is better than my dreams.*

64. **To Her:** *Sharing my life with you is a wonderful experience because there is nothing that we cannot face together, you are a treasure.*

To Him: *Every day that I spend with you is a joy. Remember that I will always give my love to you and to you alone. I will always stand by your side, even through the worst times.*

65. **To Her:** *You are my first thought in the morning. How can I make you happy, how can I make you smile. I would give you the universe if I could. So, please believe me you are more than I could ever imagine.*

To Him: *I never felt this kind of love that consumes me. Makes me feel secure, make me feel whole. I never felt that from anyone, but you. You are quite a lady.*

66. **To Her:** *I have to be honest; I look forward to seeing you at the end of a long day. You awaken my soul and I enjoy every moment of it.*

To Him: *You are the one I want to come home to; wake up to every morning. I want to see your smile, to share my happiness, sadness, frustrations and success with.*

67. **To Her:** *When I'm with you I smile more, I laugh more than I ever had. I don't feel alone when I'm with you. Instead, I feel safe and loved. You are easy to talk to. You show me that you really love me. I really appreciate you and thank you for all you have done for me.*

To Him: *Every time I see you, I fall in love all over again*

68. **To Her:** *You're like a ray of sunshine glistening on an admirable bed of roses. How delightful you are to me.*

To Him: *I have discovered that love is when the other persons happiness is more important than your own.*

69. **To Her:** *The most vital thing to me in life is knowing how to love and how to let it come in. love ourselves as we love ourselves.*

To Him: *This is a romantic journey with you. This is what makes life worth living.*

70. **To Her:** *Walk with me through life, and I promise to give you all I can for this journey.*

To Him: *I love the way you make me feel, like anything is possible. You and me baby, forever. I love you so much.*

Willie L. McClary

71. **To Her:** *You are my joy, when I'm down. My heart, my love; you're there to cheer me up with the warmth of your presence.*

To Him: *I never get enough of your love; you are nothing short of everything to me.*

72. **To Her:** *May the ring I gave you at our wedding remind you of that wonderful moment and the love we feel for each other that will last a life time.*

To Him: *I take you as my husband now and forever without reservation. I give myself freely and without conviction so that we will live our lives together as long as we both shall live.*

73. **To Her:** *You make my heart sing every time I think of you.*

To Him: *I would marry you all over again with no regrets. No one could be better than you.*

74. **To Her:** *I must speak the truth; I'm in love with you. I will not deny myself of speaking this simple truth: loving you is easy; living without you is impossible.*

To Him: *Love lets you find those hidden places that you never knew were there. You bring out the best in me. I love you.*

75. **To Her:** *I knew the second I met you that there was something about you I needed. Turned out it was just you.*

To Him: *I love you so much, nothing and nobody, not even time will change that.*

76. **To Her:** *I love you more than you will ever know my love.*

To Him: *I don't know what may happen tomorrow, all that matters now is that I'm so in love with you.*

77. **To Her:** *We have shared so many special moments together I look forward to countless others*

To Him: *I cherish you, my love.*

78. **To Her:** *You are so amazing, the great things in me are a testament to who you are.*

To Him: *You are an adventure and my lover all at once.*

79. **To Her:** *Your voice makes me smile. My love for you came with a life time guarantee.*

To Him: *I love the way you look at me. All of me love all of you. Only you can make me feel this way.*

80. **To Her:** *Life is so much better when we are together, you make me feel so good.*

To Him: *It has been about you since the day we met. How to make you smile, how can I make you happy. Loving you was one of the best things I've ever had the opportunity of experiencing.*

Willie L. McClary

81. **To Her:** *Each day I love you more, and more. Just when I though it couldn't get any better, it just happened.*

To Him: *Life is a journey, but I'm so glad that I'm with you.*

82. **To Her:** *I fell in love with the most beautiful woman in the world.*

To Him: *I love you so much, you make me reach for more. You bring peace to my mind. That's what I hope to give to you in return.*

83. **To Her:** *My heart is yours, and always will be. A paradise is when I'm with you, you make me forget every bad situation I faced today. A perfect girl; my patience has paid off.*

To Him: *Your love is like the lamp in the window that guides me home through the darkest night.*

84. **To Her:** *I vow to love you, to say goodnight, to kiss you on the lips, to have and adore especially when you feel down. At any time in any place, I want to be by your side.*

To Him: *Marriage is a symphony of grace. Orchestrated by almighty God, reflecting his love for humanity through me and you.*

85. **To Her:** *You are the finest, loveliest, tenderest, and most beautiful person I have ever known and that is an understatement.*

To Him: *You are my sunshine after the storm. With you, I know what true love is. Now I will put all my effort in keeping you by my side until the end of time.*

86. **To Her:** *It's amazing to see you now, you are one confident and beautiful woman. You can do all things through Christ that strengthens you. Therse's no stopping you now. I am willing to support you on this journey.*

To Him: *It's amazing to see you now, handsome, brilliant, over achiever and loving. I'm so blessed to have you.*

87. **To Her:** *Counting the cost of being with you is impossible. Waking up to you and going to sleep with you on my mind is good enough for me.*

To Him: *You are the finest tree, you shelter and comfort me. You are my knight; I love you I feel so safe in your arms. Nothing harmful can get to me, because I have you to protect me. I love you so much.*

88. **To Her:** *You have been so considerate and accommodating since we started on our new journey. I look forward to always being with you.*

To Him: *Looking at love the way the world sees it is less encouraging than the way we see it. You have done more than helping me see what it means to be strong and courageous. You have shown me so much in your gestures that you know what love really is.*

89. **To Her:** *Every turn we'll take will be an entry into deeper affection and a step further to advance in our relationship.*

To Him: *You bright tone brighten up my day. My heart, when heavy, lightens with every word of wisdom you speak. You are so handsome, and wise to handle situations.*

90. **To Her:** *True love trusts at all times and believes through it all. We fight all doubts and the victory is won over the threat of our relationship breakdowns.*

To Him: *I hold hands with you this day, and I assure you that I will hang on to you forever.*

91. **To Her:** *No matter what differences we've got, we can survive through every moment. Our hearts have become knitted together.*

To Him: *Pour your love on me like a summer rain. The little showers of tenderness cannot compare with the showers of affection you pour on me.*

92. **To Her:** *It's easy to differentiate between natural and artificial. You have been naturally loving, and I really appreciate that.*

To Him: *I look through your exterior and see what's inside. I have the most tender-hearted, caring man. I love you so much.*

93. **To Her:** *I've never felt like this, you awoke my love for you. You are breathtaking I have rivers of love flowing out of my heart for you. Thank you for coming into my life.*

To Him: *This energy that we have for each other is intoxicating, refreshing, and impossible to overcome. This is the love of God that we share for one another. We can achieve anything together; so glad I'm with you.*

94. **To Her:** *You are endowed with things that are uncommon to other women. You are a great woman of God.*

To Him: *You are a blessing to me as well as to others. You are loving, compassionate and cannot be duplicated you are one of a kind and I am truly blessed to have you. love you so much.*

95. **To Her:** *I really love you; I woke up this morning with you on my mind. I want to assure you no going back from here. We are taking this journey together we have started with so much determination. We'll continue to be more purposeful. Love you*

To Him: *Let's make the decision to stay true to committing ourselves to this new found love for each other. Let's strengthen each other's hand for this journey. Love you so much.*

96. **To Her:** *As your husband I promise to continue to discover new ways we complement each other with love and devotion; always.*

To Him: *I take you as my husband and vow to be honest and open to you. It is a vow I give willingly, easily, gracefully at this moment and for the rest of our lives.*

97. **To Her:** *Sweetheart as we have joined our lives together let us vow to live in truth, and to communicate fully. To hold each other against the storms of life, to feel each other's heartbeat. To you I give myself and everything that I will ever obtain in this life.*

To Him: *Wherever our journey leads us, I promise to walk with your arm and arm, hand and hand, to hold you as my husband. To learn from and to love forever.*

Willie L. McClary

98. **To Her:** *Though our beginning was small our latter end shall greatly increase (Job 8:7 KJV). We won't despise small beginnings, (Zechariah 4:10 KJV). There is so much increase to come, and you to share it with*

To Him: *The images I've projected about our relationship has been so wonderful. We are getting closer, more caring, and more loving. Our future is brighter and it starts now.*

99. **To Her:** *Loyalty, commitment, trust, and affection all spring from my heart for you. My heart has been transformed into an entity of love.*

To Him: *Not a day goes by that I'm not thinking about you, caring for you, loving you.*

100. **To Her:** *A rock solid relationship is built overtime. What matters most is how much time I have to commit to pouring my love for you into our relationship every day.*

To Him: *Marriage is so wonderful! Ordained by God so we seek him continually.*

101. **To Her:** *If I had a flower for every time I thought of you, I could walk in my garden forever.*

To Him: *I don't love you for all the things you possess, I love you because you touched my heart with your beauty and your love.*

102. **To Her:** *Let us consider how we may spur one another on toward love and good deeds. Not giving up on each other, but encourage one another.*

To Him: *I honor you, I love you, for all you have done.*

103. **To Her:** *You have captivated my heart, my bridge over troubled water. With one glare of your eyes, they melt my heart.*

To Him: *Because of your love and faithfulness to me, I praise God every day for giving me a man such as you. Love always; your wife.*

104. **To Her:** *I am your husband, and I will honor you as my wife. You are my equal partner, and God's gift for this new life.*

To Him: *As long as we love each other, God will live in us and his love will be complete in us, (1John 4:12 KJV).*

105. **To Her:** *You are the joy I sought in a relationship. I'm overwhelmed by you; graceful and beautiful you are to me. Love you always.*

To Him: *Love is the wind you can't see, but you can certainly feel.*

106. **To Her:** *I don't love you for all the things that you possess, I love you because you touched my heart with your beauty, inside and out.*

To Him: *I am infatuated with you. My heart is overwhelmed by your love and affection you give me. Thank you for all you do for me.*

Willie L. McClary

107. **To Her:** *It's hard to believe that I could marry such a woman as you. You are like no other.*

To Him: *I look at you and I see a complete man. I want to show you how much you mean to me.*

108. **To Her:** *I constantly think of you in my arms, day and night. Being with you make me feel really alive. There is so much love in my heart for you.*

To Him: *I am in love with your smile, your voice, your body, your laugh, your eyes. I am in love with all of you.*

109. **To Her:** *You can feel safe in my arms; I'll never let you go.*

To Him: *I'll never give up on you; I'll never leave you. I'll always support you and care for you. I'll forever love and cherish every moment we share together.*

110. **To Her:** *Time and time again I have to pinch myself when I see such a beautiful woman beside me. You are my dream come true.*

To Him: *So many reasons are there to love you. Your handsome, your smile, your laugh, your kind heart are some of the reasons why I love you so much.*

111. **To Her:** *I love every moment spent with you; your love has really penetrated my heart.*

To Him: *I am forever grateful for the happiness and joy you have brought into my life.*

112. **To Her:** *Today and always, I need you at my side. You are my best friend, lover, and my soulmate forever.*

To Him: *If you can see yourself the way I see you, honey, you are unstoppable, a winner, and my lover forever, love you so much.*

113. **To Her:** *I have waited all my life for you; you are my forever baby! you are the most beautiful woman I've ever seen.*

To Him: *Holding your hands gives me so much joy. Knowing that you are mine forever gives me peace.*

114. **To Her:** *Sunrises and sunsets are so much more beautiful when you came into my life. That's why I value you so much.*

To Him: *Every moment of each day, my love for you grows. You are that once in a life time dream come true.*

115. **To Her:** *I promise to love you and handle you with care. Your love conquers my heart.*

To Him: *Together we can accomplish so much more. Anything is possible!*

116. **To Her:** *I love you unconditionally; even thou we may have imperfections. You are perfect for me.*

To Him: *I love being married to you. To be found someone as special as you, were the best thing that ever happened to me.*

117. **To Her:** *The best thing we can do is to hold on to each other. Through the good times and bad. You mean the world to me; I love you so much.*

To Him: *When you realize you want to spend the rest of your life with someone, the rest of my life began the moment we met.*

118. **To Her:** *In all the world, there is no woman that can compare to you; my love!*

To Him: *When we love, we always strive to become better than we are. Everything around us becomes better too.*

119. **To Her:** *To feel the love of people who we love is a fire that feeds our life.*

To Him: *I love you for who you are, and for the man the greater man you shall become later.*

120. **To Her:** *When I saw you, I fell in love with you. You smiled because you felt it to.*

To Him: *When you really love someone, you love them in spite of their imperfections.*

121. **To Her:** *I can't promise to fix all our problems, but I can promise you want have to face them alone.*

To Him: *I want this relationship to last forever. Sweetheart, you are all I'll ever need.*

122. **To Her:** I can't get enough of you; your touch, your love, your lips. You are what I need in my life, you are the one.

To Him: The greatest thing that I've learned is to love and to be loved by someone you really care about and that's you.

123. **To Her:** No matter how faraway I am, I'll always love you. You and me together through the days and nights, I'll always love you; It will always be you.

To Him: I love you more than I have ever found a way to say to you. So, I'll just say; "I love you so much".

124. **To Her:** I look at you and I see the rest the rest of my life in front of my eyes. This is what loves feels like.

To Him: The greatest happiness of life is the conviction that we are loved; love for others, in spite of ourselves.

125. **To Her:** I'm much more when I'm with you. You help me be the best me that I can be.

To Him: The best and most beautiful things in this world cannot be seen or heard, but it can be felt and that's my love for you.

126. **To Her:** There is not one woman in the world I'd rather be with than you. For once in my life, I don't have to try to be happy when I'm with you, it just happens.

To Him: You are the inspiration behind all that I do, and you help make my life so much better. Thank you.

Willie L. McClary

127. **To Her:** *I smile every time I see you. You give me joy when I'm sad disappointed. You give me hope in times trials. That's why I love you so much.*

To Him: *I love you and I don't want to lose you. Because my life has been better since the day, I met you.*

128. **To Her:** *I was made for you, born for you; that's why I love you the way I do. The story of my life involves you.*

To Him: *I've been in love with you since the very beginning; that's why there isn't any other woman in my life that I love this way but you.*

129. **To Her:** *True love is rare, and it makes life real meaningful especially when I share life with you.*

To Him: *All that you are is all that I'll ever need.*

130. **To Her:** *I love you, and that's the beginning and end of it.*

To Him: *My love for you recognizes no barriers.*

131. **To Her:** *Our love is composed of a single soul inhabiting two bodies we are one.*

To Him: *I feel alive when we're together. Our love for each other has caught fire. I'm so in love with you.*

132. **To Her:** *If you find the woman that you really love, then hang on to her. I'll never let you go. I love you so much.*

To Him: *You really know how to love me like no one else can. Hold me like no one else can and I love every moment of it. I love you.*

133. **To Her:** *In order for me to love you properly, I need to love me. I love you because I'm happy with who I am and willing to love you the same way. I take care of me and I will take care of you. love you so much.*

To Him: *Maybe one of the greatest vows I can make to you is that I will never make you feel alone. love you so much.*

134. **To Her:** *Being deeply loved by someone gives you strength. While loving you gives me the courage to love you more.*

To Him: *Where there is love, there is life. You don't know how special you are to me.*

135. **To Her:** *The best love is the kind that awakens the soul; That makes me love you more. That gives me fire in my heart and make me reach for more. This is what I hope to give you forever.*

To Him: *You don't love someone because they're perfect; you love them in spite of the fact that they're not.*

136. **To Her:** *If I live to be a hundred years old, I'll never stop loving you.*

To Him: *I know what true love is because of you.*

Willie L. McClary

137. **To Her:** *I want this relationship to last forever. You are everything I ever wanted. You are my one and only.*

To Him: *Love freed me from the weight and pain of life that's why I love you so much.*

138. **To Her:** *From the moment I met you, I knew we were meant to be together. love you so much.*

To Him: *I can never get enough of your love.*

139. **To Her:** *I love you so much. You saw my worst and stayed. You are all I need in my life.*

To Him: *I love you more than I have ever found a way to say to you that I love you. You mean the world to me. Love you so much.*

140. **To Her:** *I just want to see you, hold you, touch you, kiss you, cuddle with you. Love you.*

To Him: *You're the only man I think about. I love you more than I ever thought possible.*

141. **To Her:** *I chose you, and will choose you over and over again. Without hesitation, without a doubt, in a heartbeat, I'll keep choosing you.*

To Him: *I love you more than the disagreements behind us. I love you more than the obstacles that could try to come between us. I love you the most.*

142. **To Her:** I want you, all of you. Your flaws, your mistakes, your imperfections. I want you and only you. There is no mistake in loving you.

To Him: If you only knew how much those little moments with you really meant to me.

143. **To Her:** The best thing that I have ever done was to give my heart to you. I love you and I am yours.

To Him: I am and I will remain utterly and completely and totally in love with you. I realized, "I will never truly love anyone the way I love you".

144. **To Her:** I fall more deeply in love with you every single day.

To Him: Every day that I'm with you is so special because you are such an awesome guy.

145. **To Her:** Give me all of you and I'll give you all of me, my love. You are everything to me.

To Him: when two people really care about each other, they always find a way to make it work. No matter how hard it is.

146. **To Her:** Only once in your life, I truly believe you find someone who can completely turn your world around. Your love helped me to heal.

To Him: I love you because you are awesome you found me in pieces and lead me to peace.

147. **To Her:** Good byes are only for those who love with their eyes because for those who love with their heart and soul there is no such thing as separation.

To Him: You're the one I truly love. I can't get enough of you.

148. **To Her:** I will never stop trying to make you happy. When you find the one you love you never give up.

To Him: When I see you smile, I see someone more beautiful than the stars. That's why I love you so much.

149. **To Her:** All that you are is all I'll ever need.

To Him: I want all of you; forever you and me.

150. **To Her:** I love the way you make me feel like anything is possible, and that life is worth living.

To Him: You are truly a great guy. I love you.

151. **To Her:** You make me want to be a better man. You are as good as it gets, thank you.

To Him: With the whole world crumbling, the love we have for each other will never die.

152. **To Her:** It seems right now that all I've ever done in my life was making my way to you. I'm so grateful for you.

To Him: You are my best friend; I feel more alive now that we are together.

153. **To Her:** *You always know exactly how to express your love to me in more ways than one. And I am absolutely head over heels in love with you; sweetheart.*

To Him: *Only once in your life, "I truly believe", you find someone as special as you.*

154. **To Her:** *I knew the minute I met you I wanted to spend the rest of my life with you. I love you.*

To Him: *My heart will always be yours, my affection will always be yours, my hugs will always be yours. All of me is yours.*

155. **To Her:** *We have chemistry baby; we are so much better together. The sky is the limit for us, together forever.*

To Him: *The way I feel about you is like a heartbeat, soft and persistent underlying everything.*

156. **To Her:** *No matter how broken we were no matter how many challenges we face we will fight our way out together. Because that's what we do, we never give up.*

To Him: *You are my priest, you pray for me, you intercede for me when I was down and I didn't know what to do. Thank you for being by my side.*

157. **To Her:** *We have the rest of our lives together. Every day I will express my love for you. I'm positive that the path that we are headed on is wonderful. I want to say I love you; I love you; I love you.*

To Him: *No matter what happens I will never stop loving you. I will always be here for you, I promise.*

158. **To Her:** *Unlike any woman I'd ever met, you make my heart beats faster whenever I'm around you; even when I think of you. My love for you has no end.*

To Him: *You are the most gracious, bravest, compassionate man that I know. There will never be another like you and now that you realize that you know this. I will never let you go.*

159. **To Her:** *You are the most incredible woman that I have ever met, the most beautiful I had ever seen. Every time I close my eyes, I see your pretty face. There is no doubt in my mind you are the one for me.*

To Him: *It was the intimacy of shared secrets, the unconditional acceptance of who I am. It was the confidence in knowing no matter what happened that you would always be there for me.*

160. **To Her:** *It's the first sparks of love and attraction. It was like a warm summer breeze; goose bumps on my arms. It was like adding sweetness to my soul. Something so new and tender, so delicate.*

To Him: *Our love for each other flows like a river. Now that I've known a life with you by my side, I could never be without you.*

161. **To Her:** *You've reminded me to live: You are my star that shines so brightly. Instead, of disappearing, you make me feel alive. You draw out the boldness that was inside of me.*

To Him: *I'll give you all of me my darling, our hearts are bound together. We are the best together. Fearless, daring and bold, we are one.*

162. **To Her:** *You are dearer to me than you would ever know. I think of your kisses, your understanding heart; you're my favorite person in the world.*

To Him: *I never loved you more than I do right now. you're one incredible man. I'm forever grateful.*

163. **To Her:** *I want to love on you throughout the day. Holding you in my arms, I want to know every part of your sexy body; your lips, your curves, all of you. Love allows wants to find those hidden places. Those places you would not have shown otherwise.*

To Him: *All that you are is all I will ever need.*

164. **To Her:** *My life would not be complete without you. I vow to always love you.*

To Him: *You will forever be mine, always.*

165. **To Her:** *You are my queen, lovely lady.*

To Him: *There is never enough of me loving you.*

166. **To Her:** *Let's keep love in our hearts for one another. A life without it is like a sunless garden when the flowers are dead.*

To Him: *Love is like beautiful flowers whose fragrance make the garden a place of delight.*

167. **To Her:** *Being deeply loved by you gives me strength, and courage to love you more.*

To Him: *Love is eternal, the aspect may change, but not the essence.*

168. **To Her:** *Our love is composed of a single soul living in two bodies*

To Him: *Love is when the other person's happiness is more important than your own.*

169. **To Her:** *There is nothing more important than having you as my best friend.*

To Him: *You are the song that my heart wants to sing. Over and over again.*

170. **To Her:** *What a treasure I have found in you.*

To Him: *Love isn't something you find. Love found me when you came along.*

171. **To Her:** *I love you more than I have the words to say.*

To Him: *Bravery is to love unconditionally without expecting anything in return.*

172. **To Her:** *Anyone can catch my eyes, but it takes someone special, "like you", to capture my heart.*

To Him: *What we have is so special through all of life's challenges. We have decided to pray together and allow God to do a work in us. I love you so much.*

173. **To Her:** *I may not have been your first love, your first date, but I promise you I will be your last everything.*

To Him: *Long after the chocolate is eaten, the flowers are faded away, I'll continue loving you.*

174. **To Her:** *Love recognizes no barriers, it jumps hurdles, run through walls to be with the one you love.*

To Him: *We're lovers, companions, best friends, and partners. For me it's loving you more and more.*

175. **To Her:** *Real relationships are built overtime and by working hard at it.*

To Him: *I consider myself to be the happiest woman in the world, because I've found a real gem, and that's you.*

176. **To Her:** *We both won because we have each other; how wonderful.*

To Him: *It doesn't get any better than this; you and me forever.*

177. **To Her:** *Today is a new day and we have great expectations with the help of God we will conquer it together.*

To Him: *No doubt, God will exceed our expectations as we look to him for guidance this very day.*

178. **To Her:** *When I look into your eyes, I see confidence, I see a woman of strength and courage. You are my queen.*

To Him: *I believe in you and I appreciate you, for all you have done for me. I love you.*

179. **To Her:** *I love watching the sunrise with you holding me in my arms. Me running my fingers through your hair, it's priceless.*

To Him: *The feel of you embracing me just makes me want more of you.*

180. **To Her:** *Our journey has been a true love story. I'm so glad to share it with such an understanding and loving person. You're a rare jewel.*

To Him: *Wow! You still amaze me with your love, that's personalize just for me; how special.*

181. **To Her:** *You make me smile every morning I wake up. I constantly think of you. You are so irresistible. I desire you more and more.*

To Him: *Come with me to our secret place, just you and me. I'll lead the way.*

182. **To Her:** *Life gets a little messy sometimes, but we always come up with brilliant ideals that totally take our minds to a place of serenity. I love you so much.*

To Him: *I promise to love you the rest of my life, you and no other.*

183. **To Her:** *You are my first true love and you will be my last.*

To Him: *You're on my mind throughout the day that's how special you are to me.*

184. **To Her:** *Hello beautiful! Another day to share my love with you.*

To Him: *Hello handsome! Let's start the day with a little romance.*

185. **To Her:** *The single most extraordinary thing I've done with my life is fall in love with you. You hold the keys to my heart.*

To Him: *Our true destiny lies within us. We cannot do alone; we find it within each other.*

186. **To Her:** *Suddenly, every love song was about you. I'm deeply in love with you.*

To Him: *You show me what true love is day by day with the way you hold me, kiss me, cherished me; every time we are together.*

187. **To Her:** *In this world, there is no heart for me like yours. In all the world, there is no love for you like mine.*

To Him: *You are the best husband ever. No one could ever hold me like you and satisfy my every desire like you do.*

188. **To Her:** *You are truly a great woman of God, always pouring into the lives of others. What a gift you are to all of us.*

To Him: *You are a man of great knowledge and Godly wisdom.*

189. **To Her:** *Life is wonderful since you came into my life. This is the beauty of finding a partner that you really love, because after all the highs and lows and ups and downs, we have each other. Which makes the journey worthwhile.*

To Him: *When I see your face, there is not a thing that I would change because you are amazing just the way you are.*

190. **To Her:** *In one respect I have succeeded as gloriously as anyone who's ever lived: I've loved you with all my heart and soul; and to me, this is true success.*

To Him: *Immature love says: I love you because I need you. Mature love says I need you, because I love you.*

191. **To Her:** *You are the finest, loveliest, tenderest and most beautiful person I have ever known. But even that is an understatement.*

To Him: *Love doesn't just sit there like a stone it makes things happen. Love makes life worth living.*

192. **To Her:** *Every moment spent with you is my favorite part of the day.*

To Him: *When I met you, you made me forget about yesterday and dream about tomorrow.*

193. **To Her:** *I love you more than I can ever find a way to say, "I love you".*

To Him: *Every love story is beautiful, but ours is my favorite.*

194. **To Her:** *When I found you, the search was over. I've found my true love.*

To Him: *You found parts of me I didn't knew existed, and in you I found a love I never knew existed.*

195. **To Her:** *Your love is like a lamp in the window that guides me home at night.*

To Him: *Distance between me and you are not at all an issue because I have you in my heart.*

196. **To Her:** *Love me without restrictions, trust me without fear, want me always and accept me for who I am.*

To Him: *If you only knew the impact you have on my life. I'm so glad you're a part of my life.*

197. **To Her:** *True love doesn't mean being inseparable; it means being separated and nothing changes.*

To Him: *I want to be the girl who makes your bad days better, and the one that makes you say, "my life has really change since I met her".*

198. **To Her:** *You are not only my true love; you are my life.*

To Him: *I want to be in your arms where you hold me tight.*

199. **To Her:** *This is a relationship I want to last forever; my love.*

To Him: *You are my prince, and my hero, my heart, my baby. You are my everything.*

200. **To Her:** *That's how you know you love someone, when you can't experience anything great without the other person there to share it with you.*

To Him: *I fell in love with the way you touch me, without using your hands.*

201. **To Her:** *I cannot lose you, because if I did, I'd have lost my best friend, my soulmate, my smile, my laugh, my everything.*

To Him: *Your hands fit mine like it's made just for me.*

202. **To Her:** *A real man never stop trying to show his woman how much she means to him years after they are married.*

To Him: *No matter how many times we disagree, I'm never going to stop loving you. I will keep my promise to you and never give up on you; I promise.*

203. **To Her:** *I remember the day I ask you to marry me and make me the happiest guy in the world.*

To Him: *I was so happy, with tears in my eyes; I happily said, "yes".*

204. **To Her:** *Every day with the one I love is to be cherished.*

To Him: *Love cures all ills. Both the ones who give it, and the one who receives it.*

205. **To Her:** *The sweetest of all sounds is the voice of the woman who says, "I'm in love with you".*

To Him: *You replace memories of bad relationships with the sweetest dreams; my worries with happiness, and my fears with love.*

206. **To Her:** *You make my heart joyful when I'm with you.*

To Him: *There is no bad consequences to loving you. With all my heart, I love you.*

207. **To Her:** *All that you are is all I will ever need*

To Him: *Being married to you is like having someone in your corner to love at all times.*

208. **To Her:** *When we truly love, we always strive to become better than we are. When we strive to become better than we are everything around us becomes better too.*

To Him: *The real lover is the man who can thrill you by kissing your forehead, smiling and looking into your eyes.*

209. **To Her:** *I want you forever, every day; You and my always.*

To Him: *Two people in love, together, living in this world. That's a beautiful life.*

210. **To Her:** *All I want is to pursue beautiful dreams with you.*

To Him: *Love never fails; you are so amazing. The way you demonstrate your love for me is simply breath taking.*

211. **To Her:** *You are the definition of what a real wife is supposed to be.*

To Him: *Sometimes the smallest things shine brightest in our lives. It's the little things you do mean so much to me.*

212. **To Her:** *You have my heart for the rest of our lives.*

To Him: *You will forever be my true love.*

213. **To Her:** *All of me love all of you; I love you endlessly.*

To Him: *You are my one and only, you are my everything.*

214. **To Her:** *You never fail to amaze me. Every day there is something new that makes me love you even more than the day before.*

To Him: *You mean the world to me; Thank you for all that you do.*

215. **To Her:** *I really do love you; I've found the love of my life and my closest truest friend.*

To Him: *You make my heart sing; I'm so happy when I am with you. love you so much.*

216. **To Her:** *There is a fire of love for you burning inside of me for you. My love for you is endless; I Love you with all my heart.*

To Him: *You are the flame that keeps me heart lit day after day.*

Willie L. McClary

217. **To Her:** *My eyes will always be for you. I could only love you more than I did yesterday. I love showing you how much I love you.*

To Him: *You give me the kind of feeling that you could only read about in novels. I look at you and see the one I love and will be with for the rest of my life.*

218. **To Her:** *You will always feel safe in my arms; I will never let you go. love you so much.*

To Him: *I love snuggling with you. Our chemistry is simply amazing.*

219. **To Her:** *I'll never let you go; I'll never leave you. I'll forever love and cherish our relationship. love you so much.*

To Him: *Time and time again you make my heart skip a beat. You know me all too well. Keep doing what you do to me.*

220. **To Her:** *There are so many reasons to love you. Your beautiful smile, your laugh, your heart. That's what make me love you more and more.*

To Him: *I love every moment spent with you. Your love has touched my heart.*

221. **To Her:** *I am forever grateful for the love, joy, and happiness you have brought into my life. What a lady!*

To Him: *I need you beside me always. You are my love, my covering and my soul mate.*

222. **To Her:** *If you could only see yourself the way I see you. You are absolutely stunning.*

To Him: *And to think that I have been waiting all of my life for you, that what makes me get up in the morning just to see your handsome face.*

223. **To Her:** *Sunrises and sunsets have become so much more beautiful ever since I met you.*

To Him: *Every hope, every dream that I have is inspired by you. Thank you for encouraging me to do my very best love you.*

224. **To Her:** *You are one in a lifetime dream come true. Every time I see you, I fall in love all over again.*

To Him: *I promise to handle you with care and treasure you with love, I promise.*

225. **To Her:** *Your smile conquers my heart; I will never leave you alone. I will always be here for you, no matter what happens. love you so much.*

To Him: *You're on my mind day and night; thinking of ways to make you even happier.*

226. **To Her:** *Today we will continue where we left off yesterday. Only to be better in our walk of life; I only want the very best for you.*

To Him: *I cherish every day with you, not taking one moment for granted. Because you deserve the very best.*

227. To Her: *Sweetheart, you are so special to me. I love spending quality time with you.*

To Him: *I can't help but blush when I see you, I'm reminded of so many memorable moments.*

228. To Her: *My angel, my heart, my life, my world, you're the one that I want, the one that I need. I'm yours always my love; my everything.*

To Him: *I love you more than words can explain. I love you because you understand me. You took time to teach me, support me, and encourage me. Thank you so much.*

229. To Her: *Time and time again I have to pinch myself when I you're next to me. You are my dream come true.*

To Him: *The chances of me finding a woman like you is once in a life time. Miracles do happen.*

230. To Her: *You are my love, my joy, my happiness. You are extraordinary, exquisite, impressive, and beautiful.*

To Him: *I hope you know that that every time I tell you get home safe, stay warm, have a nice day, and sleep well. What I'm really trying to say is, "that I love You so much that words can even explain how I feel about you".*

231. **To Her:** *There isn't one person in the world that I want more than you.*

To Him: *There's something about you that I'm not willing to lose, because I know I want find it in anyone else.*

232. **To Her:** *Not long ago I was alone, and then you came along. Now, I'm home with the woman I love. To Him: Please don't doubt my love for you; it's the one thing I'm sure of.*

233. **To Her:** *There's something special about you. I don't want to lose you because I know I would never find it in anyone else.*

To Him: *You give me the kind of feeling that novels are written about.*

234. **To Her:** *I know that I'm in love because my reality is better than my dreams.*

To Him: *There are two instances that I want to be with you: That's now and forever.*

235. **To Her:** *You are far more amazing, beautiful, loving, kind, woman in the world.*

To Him: *Everyone has something they are addicted too, mine just happen to be you.*

Willie L. McClary

236. **To Her:** *If I had a flower for every time, I thought of you, I could walk through my garden forever*

To Him: *I want to be the best woman you've ever met; loving, kind, that make you forget about the rest.*

237. **To Her:** *Now I know where I belong, and that's right here with you.*

To Him: *I found my home and paradise; it's here with you.*

238. **To Her:** *My dream came true the moment I met you. I really believe you are the best thing that ever happen to me.*

To Him: *Making memories with you is my favorite thing to do.*

239. **To Her:** *You're that once in a life time dream come true. Your love conquers my heart. To Him: I'm happier than I've ever been in my life. My love for you will never end.*

240. **To Her:** *You are my everything. Always have, always will be.*

To Him: *I wish I could watch you every second of the day. The love that I have for you leave me speechless.*

241. **To Her:** *Life with you is tranquil yet full of surprises and I am in it for the long haul.*

To Him: *You captivated my heart. You more to me than you could ever imagine.*

242. Her: I feel much more complete when I'm with you. You are my forever confidant. My love for you will never die.

To Him: It's your beauty within that I find so attractive. Your love for me is overwhelming.

243. To Her: I love you and I will love you until I die. I'd rather spend one moment holding you than a lifetime knowing I never could.

To Him: Loving you was never an option, it is a necessity.

244. To Her: I would only get one chance to fall in love with a woman like you. You are my heart, my life, my everything.

To Him: You make me happy no one else can.

245. To Her: Babe, you make me feel wonderful, and loved. You make me a better person, and I don't want to live my life without you by my side.

To Him: When you're with someone you love, you never wonder when is the best time to kiss them; you just do it when you feel like it. I think now is the right time. I love you so much.

246. To Her: Every day I wonder, "have I done enough to show you how much I love you"?

To Him: You're my baby, my love, my happiness, my joy, my everything.

247. To Her: *I fell in love with you with my eyes wide open. Choosing you to be by my side every step of the way*

To Him: *I love looking into your eyes as we hold hands. Your smile, your touch, makes me feel so special and great. The feeling I get when I wrap my arms around you, is hard to explain. I just want to be with you.*

248. To Her: *I love all of you. If I could give you one thing is the ability to see you through my eyes. Only then would you realize how special you are to me.*

To Him: *I want to be your choice, and your answer. I never want to be your question. You are my soul mate; someone you can trust and depend on.*

249. To Her: *I love the way you call me, the way you tease me, the way you embrace me, the way you care for me. I love you just the way you are.*

To Him: *The two greatest days of my life is when I was born again, and the day I met you. You have always been my true love.*

250. To Her: *Our connection is too strong to break. Trust me when I say our love is more than just a simple word to me. It's so real that it is a part of who we are. Our love is so intense that I can't get enough of it.*

To Him: *I feel safe when I'm falling asleep in your arms. Listening to your heartbeat slowly puts me to sleep. Knowing that everything is ok as long as I'm with you.*

251. **To Her:** *Some relationships lasts long not because it was destined to be, but because two people have decided to keep fighting for it.*

To Him: *No matter how many years pass by, there is one thing that will always be permanent. And that's your place next to me.*

252. **To Her:** *There is only one true love story in our lifetime that is unlike any other. This kind of love that I feel for you will never be extinguished. It's fire that will burn throughout eternity.*

To Him: *All that you are is all I'll ever need.*

253. **To Her:** *I look at everyday with you as a gift from God.*

To Him: *Being married to you is like having someone in my corner all the time, it feels great.*

254. **To Her:** *Let's always greet each other with a smile and a kiss. Let's keep love in our hearts, burning.*

To Him: *You are my always and forever. So many reasons there are to love you. Your smile, your laugh, your kind heart. I am forever grateful for the joy you have brought into my life.*

255. **To Her:** *You may not be perfect, but you are perfect for me, and that's all that matters.*

To Him: *One of the most important things in my life is to love and be loved by you.*

Willie L. McClary

256. To Her: I couldn't love you more than I do right now. I can't get enough of loving you.

To Him: Sometimes I find myself staring at you. Just admiring how beautiful you really are.

257. To Her: True love stories never ends. Your love makes life worth living.

To Him: You are my best friend, my lover, my everything. Love was a choice I made the moment I met you.

258. To Her: The best person for me to hold on to in life is you. You are irresistible; Can't stop loving you.

To Him: I fell in love with your courage, your sincerity, and yourself respect. That's the reason that I'm here with you. You love me the way you love yourself.

259. To Her: My heart joyful when you take my hand; my love grows stronger as we embrace each other. Because of you I am better person now that we are together.

To Him: In this world there is no heart for me but yours. No one could love you more than I could.

260. To Her: Love has nothing to do with what I am expecting to get-only with what I am expecting to give. That is my everything.

To Him: Being deeply loved by you give me strength, and courage to love you the even more.

261. **To Her:** *If I know what true love is, it's because of you. Your love is irresistible.*

To Him: *Love is that condition in which the happiness of another person is essential to your own.*

262. **To Her:** *If God planned you for me and me for you, then nothing can separate you from me and me from you.*

To Him: *Since love grows within you, so beauty grows. For love is the beauty of our souls.*

263. **To Her:** *The love that I have for you cannot be measured. Intense love does not measure, it just gives.*

To Him: *We need to love without getting tired, be faithful in small things, because love is where our strength lies.*

264. **To Her:** *The best expression of love is the time that we share together. The best time to love is now.*

To Him: *Love pays attention to the smallest matters in your life. Listen to your cares, your fears, your doubts. I accept you the way Jesus accepted me.*

265. **To Her:** *To love means, to love you the way God intended you to be loved.*

To Him: *I'm not looking for you to fill my tank in a way that only God can do. A marriage cannot survive if I only think of myself. We need to recognize that to love you is a choice that I made no matter what I go through.*

Willie L. McClary

266. To Her: *A good marriage is the union of two who are willing to forgive.*

To Him: *When I say, "I love you"; I don't mean only when things are good, I love you through it all. The good and the bad. Because that's how Christ loves me.*

267. To Her: *God chose you not because you are perfect, but because you are perfect for me.*

To Him: *Of all the gifts God gave me, the greatest gift is you.*

268. To Her: *The kind of love that we have make others say, "that's God's love right there"!*

To Him: *Where love is, God is. Love gives us the power to transcend our limitations and fears.*

269. To Her: *Faith makes all things possible. Love makes giving to you easy.*

To Him: *Being loved by you is life's second greatest blessing; loving you is makes me know how blessed I am.*

270. To Her: *The person that God me may not be perfect, but you will always provide me with the love I needed.*

To Him: *When we love God first, we love each other better.*

271. **To Her:** *There's no time to hate when you love. Let's fall in love with God first. Then we can love each other better.*

To Him: *I prayed for the greatest person to come into my life — for love and friendship. And God gave me you.*

272. **To Her:** *Real Love, instinctively desires permanence. Love never fails.*

To Him: *Where Love is, God is.*

273. **To Her:** *For me to deeply love you transcend my limitations and fears for the woman I love.*

To Him: *Faith makes all things possible, Love makes all things easier.*

274. **To Her:** *Being loved is the second greatest blessing; loving is the greatest. To Him: Love has the qualities that becomes stronger as times passes*

275. **To Her:** *God has given us the gift of love to understand what true love is and how we should love one another.*

To Him: *I want to write a love story with you, just as God wrote one with me when he gave me you.*

276. **To Her:** *If God deemed me worthy of his love, then there is no excuse for me not to love you as well.*

To Him: *Even in your darkest days, I will still love you. I chose you to love and to cherish.*

277. To Her: Imagine a man so focused on God the only time he looked up is to see you because he heard God say, "That's her".

To Him: It's ok to love each other; It's what makes us strong, it's what makes us human.

278. To Her: I love you so much; I'm happier now because I have you

To Him: In all the world there is no heart for me like yours. In all the world there is no love for you like mine.

279. To Her: Until my last days, I'll always love you.

To Him: I'm in Paradise whenever we are together.

280. For Her: material things are no replacement for my love for you.

For Him: Love is the doorway through which we pass from selfishness to service.

281. To Her: To love means to see you the way God intended for me to.

To Him: Love is not only something you feel, it's something you do.

282. To Her: Nothing can bring a real sense of security into our home but trust and true love.

To Him: Great marriages don't happen by luck or by accident. They are the result of consistent investment of time, thoughtfulness, forgiveness, affection, prayer, mutual respect, and a rock-solid commitment between us.

283. To Her: *Marriage is sharing your life with your best friend, and enjoying the journey along the way.*

To Him: *A marriage cannot survive when we think only of ourselves. True love is about giving not receiving.*

284. To Her: *Our love recognizes no barriers. It jumps over hurdles, leap fences, penetrates walls to arrive at its destination.*

To Him: *Love is patient and kind, does not envy, is not arrogant or rude. Does not insist on its own way; it is not irritable or resentful; Love bears all things, hope for the best, endures all things. Love never fails, (1 cor. 13:4-8 ESV).*

285. To Her: *God's Word is the perfect roadmap for a great marriage, and those who live by his Word will reap the blessings that obedience brings.*

To Him: *Put on then, as God's chosen ones, holy and beloved, compassionate hearts, kindness, humility, meekness, patience, bearing with one another, and if there is a complaint against another, forgiving each other; as the Lord has forgiven you, (Colossians 3:12-13 ESV).*

286. To Her: *I want our marriage to look less like the world, and more like Christ.*

To Him: *As a wife I chose to honor you, because I love you.*

287. **To Her:** *What we faced was intended to strengthen our marriage, not destroy it.*

To Him: *I want to know you fully, love you unconditionally, to respect you always, to give, to embrace you closely. This is the gift of marriage.*

288. **To Her:** *A great marriage looks to the future, not the past.*

To Him: *What God has joined together, let no one separate.*

299. **To Her:** *Oh girl, let's be adventurers!*

To Him: *God doesn't want me to fix you, God want me to love you.*

300. **To Her:** *I know that you were put on this earth just for me. That's why I never want to be apart.*

To Him: *Love is that condition in which your happiness is essential to mine.*

301. **To Her:** *You found parts of me I never knew existed, and in you I found a love I no longer believed was real.*

To Him: *Love does not dominate; it cultivates.*

302. To Her: *The greatest happiness in life is to know that you are loved in spite of ourselves.*

To Him: *Love consist of us walking in the same direction.*

303. To Her: *My Love for you is a fire that burns deep in me.*

To Him: *Love is an emotion sent from heaven. An irresistible desire to embrace, to kiss, to hold you.*

304. To Her: *The giving of love is an education within itself. We are most alive when we love.*

To Him: *The only thing I never get enough of is your love.*

305. To Her: *To love and be loved is to feel the sun from both sides.*

To Him: *Our love composed of a single soul inhabiting two bodies.*

306. To Her: *I want to be your favorite place to go when you've had a bad or good day.*

To Him: *You deserve to never guess how much you mean to me.*

307. To Her: *My life slowly began to change for the better the moment I met you.*

To Him: *Even though we never said it, we knew the moment we met; that you were the one for me.*

308. To Her: *You were always mine, I just had to fine you.*

To Him: *You are exactly, precisely, and perfectly what I needed in my life.*

309. To Her: *Sometimes you can't explain what you see in a person. It's just the way they take you to a place where no one else can.*

To Him: *I have looked at you in many ways and I want to love you in every way.*

310. To Her: *I'm madly in love with you. You are forever mine.*

To Him: *I have never felt so calm yet on fire. All at the same time when I'm with you. You are the one I've been waiting for all my life.*

311. To Her: *I fell for you when I first saw you, and I'm still falling for you.*

To Him: *You're my waking thoughts, my sweet dreams, and everything in between.*

312. To Her: *You walked into my life like you always lived there-; like my heart was a home built just for you.*

To Him: *I have a man who loves me through my fears. Trust me from a distance and with me in my heart every single day.*

313. **To Her:** I always wanted you. Before I knew what I wanted, it was you. I saw my home in your eyes; I found love in your smile.

To Him: And then I saw you, oh, there you are. I've been waiting for you.

314. **To Her:** Asleep or awake, I dream of you all the same.

To Him: You are the idea I ever had about love.

315. **To Her:** when you meet the right person, it's simple. You never question it, because you know the answer is yes.

To Him: I searched for affection in shallow places. I gave people a chance that did not deserve it. But once I stop trying to find the right one, then you came into my life.

316. **To Her:** I promise there hasn't been a day that I stopped wanting you and you haven't gotten out of my head at all since I first met you.

To Him: What was meant to be will always find a way.

317. **To Her:** I may never find the words beautiful enough to describe all that you mean to me, but I will spend the rest of my life searching for them.

To Him: I just want to thank you, not for just being in my life and for sticking around, but for reminding me that even broken things can be loved.

318. **To Her:** *You are every beautiful thing that has ever happened to me, wrapped in a person. You may think you are ordinary, but to me you are exceptional.*

To Him: *You walked into my life like you belong there. Took down my walls and sparked fire of love in my heart.*

319. **To Her:** *A man's strength is measured by the way he will protect the heart of the woman he loves.*

To Him: *I fell in love with someone who is my safe place and my biggest defender.*

320. **To Her:** *My heart has waited so long to be loved by someone like you.*

To Him: *You are a mixer of everything I had ever wanted.*

321. **To Her:** *I've realized that real love comes down to feel safe enough to be vulnerable.*

To Him: *You really get me. You encourage me and help me push past my flaws. To me you're everything I need.*

322. **To Her:** *I am not the best, but I promise that I will always love you.*

To Him: *With your body pressed close to mine I say, "Pull me closer".*

323. To Her: We are going to have a beautiful life together. It's so hard to put into words what you mean to me. I love you like I've never loved anyone else.

To Him: One of the first signs of real love is the moment you realize they are trying their best to understand you.

324. To Her: A woman can't change a man because she loves him, a man changes himself because he loves her.

To Him: Baby, thank you for coming into my life.

325. To Her: When I say that I love you, I'm reminding you that you are my life.

To Him: I love how you take care of me. How you keep working to be a better man. Even on days I fail to be a better woman.

326. To Her: It's a beautiful thing when you get so comfortable with someone that you can tell them things you've never told anyone else before.

327. To Her: In you I've found everything that I would ever need.

To Him: My life would not be complete without you.

328. To Her: With one kiss you know all I haven't said.

To Him: Your smile melts my heart. I can't believe you are mine.

329. To Her: You are my greatest adventure.

To Him: I wish that I could turn back time. I'd find you sooner and love you longer.

330. To Her: True love never dies; it gets stronger over time.

To Him: Having you is having all I ever need.

331. To Her: You are exactly the one I prayed for and the one I dreamed of.

To Him: I can't help it; every day I fall more and more in love with you.

332. To Her: Our love is worth fighting for.

To Him: I am my beloved and my beloved is mine, (Song of Solomon 6:3 KJV).

333. To Her: There is no fear in love, (1 John 4:18 KJV).

To Him: some people have searched their whole life to find what I have found in you.

334. To Her: what we have can never be replaced.

To Him: Love you yesterday, love you still, and I always will.

335. To Her: *Love takes off the mask we feared we could not live without.*

To Him: *Love is known more in deeds than words.*

336. To Her: *Love is that condition in which the happiness of another is essential to your own.*

To Him: *Love is like the wind you can't see it, but you can feel it.*

337. To Her: *I will continue to share my heart with the woman I love.*

To Him: *There are many reasons why I love you. There are so many I can't count them all.*

338. To Her: *Love does not dominate; it cultivates.*

To Him: *The only thing I never get enough of is your love.*

339. To Her: *You always gain by giving love.*

To Him: *My love for you has no barriers.*

340. To Her: *To me you are perfectly made just for me.*

To Him: *There's nothing that I would not do to make you feel loved.*

Willie L. McClary

341. **To Her:** *There's nothing that I would not do to make you feel my love.*

To Him: *Love is something sent from heaven. No one has loved me the way you do.*

342. **To Her:** *The best thing to do in this life is to hold on to each other, and never let go.*

To Him: *You should be held, and kissed often by the one that love you, and that's me.*

343. **To Her:** *Personally, I love a great love story that involves me and you.*

To Him: *Love is like a flower, just let it grow and become even more beautiful.*

344. **To Her:** *To find a good wife is special. This much is true, I was blessed the moment I met you.*

To Him: *No one can measure, not even poets, how much love I have for you.*

345. **To Her:** *All that we have enjoyed as a couple we can never lose. All that we love to do together is a part of what make our relationship so special.*

To Him: *Let's throw caution to the wind and give all we can to make this relationship even more special.*

346. To Her: You, as much as anyone, deserve my love and affection.

To Him: Love is shown more in deeds than in words alone.

347. To Her: Love is such a powerful force. My love is always there for you to embrace-that kind of unconditional love that's willing to go all the way with you.

To Him: There's all kinds of reasons that I fell in love with you. Timing was everything. You found me when I needed you most.

348. To Her: When I found you, I never want to be apart from you.

To Him: Real love is romantic. I want you to feel what I feel.

349. To Her: Loving me is loving you. I could never get enough of loving you.

To Him: I want all of you, right now and forever.

350. To Her: Love is an endless act of forgiveness.

To Him: In all the world there is no love like mine. No one can love you like I can.

351. To Her: You are the light that aluminates my path. The love and change you brought into my life are truly unforgettable. Thanks, my love.

To Him: When I look at you, I wonder did I do something extraordinary to get such a gift from God. You have been such a blessing in my life and I just want to say that I love you.

Willie L. McClary

352. **To Her:** *No matter how many years pass by in our marriage, there are will be two moments when I will like to be with you-now and forever! Love you, sweetie.*

To Him: *You are a special gift from heaven. Your smile warms my heart and your presence makes me whole. I love you today and forever.*

353. **To Her:** *You are the most gorgeous woman that I've ever seen. You melt my heart when you look into my eyes. I'm so in love with you; I've got to have you now and forever.*

To Him: *I love looking into your eyes. They calm me down after a stressful day at work; I love you so much.*

354. **To Her:** *You are thoughtful and understanding; you are so much fun to be around. But most of all, I'm glad that you are my wife.*

To Him: *You are my answered prayer, my heart desired, my dream realized. I Love you so much.*

355. **To Her:** *My gratitude for having you is only surpassed by my amazement at the joy you give me.*

To Him: *Having a husband like you, made me realized how blessed I am. You are one in ten million. I love you much.*

356. **To Her:** *I can never be sad when I'm around you. Thanks for truly being there for me; my beautiful wife. I love you!*

To Him: *With a husband like you, I'm so blessed. You are always on my mind. My beloved; you are certainly in a class by yourself.*

357. **To Her:** *Nothing in my life has ever meant as much to me as you do. I am so grateful that you are my wife. I want to fill your life with happiness and love.*

To Him: *My love for you has increased over time. I'm thankful that you are mine. If I forget to say it, "You mean the world to me".*

358. **To Her:** *Fights and arguments, ups and down. Hugs and kisses, smiles and frowns. We'll make it through it all together. Not just now, but forever. I love you.*

To Him: *To be your husband was all I ever wanted; to be yours forever was all could ever dream of.*

359. **To Her:** *You give me hope in the times of trials, joy in my sadness, love in all that you do.*

To Him: *You hold my hand for a while, but you have my heart forever. I Love you!*

360. **To Her:** *I believe in you completely; you are my best friend. Just when I thought that I couldn't love you anymore, you prove me wrong. I'm thankful that you are my wife.*

To Him: *I fall short of words to tell you how much you mean to me. All I can say is my life is so much better now that we are together. You are the husband of my dreams.*

361. **To Her:** *No matter how challenging my day has been, I know that I'm coming home to the most beautiful woman that I had ever seen. I love you so much.*

To Him: *Every day with you is better than the day before. How is it that you can continuously improve upon your perfection? I love you more than you could ever dream of.*

362. **To Her:** *In this ever-changing world, you are a constant friend to me. I would be lost without you.*

To Him: *We've been together for so long through the thick and the thin. I can't imagine my life without you. I couldn't ask for more than you have given me this far in our marriage. Thank you for being you!*

363. **To Her:** *No one will ever come beyond you; you're a perfect wife for me. I couldn't ask for more; you are so beautiful to me.*

To Him: *Every time I look at you, you remind me of how much God truly loves me. He gave me the most wonderful gift in the world. That's You!*

364. **To Her:** *I know I'm not the perfect husband, but I promise that I will love you and stay faithful to you for the rest of my life.*

To Him: *I'm so blessed to have an affectionate and caring husband. I've never been so happy until I met you.*

365. To Her: *All my days and nights are filled with wonders and amazements. Let me announce that you are the world greatest wife; special and wonderful you are to me. I love you so much.*

To Him: *You help guide me through my dark days; you are the support behind my success. A special thanks to a special husband; Love you so much!*

Conclusion

Express your love to your partner and most importantly touch his or her hearts when you put your feelings into words. This book has the prefect collection of quotes for a husband and a wife to dedicate their love and affection to one another. "Let love and faithfulness never leave you; bind them about around your neck, write them the tablets of your hearts. Then you will find favor and a good name in the sight of God and man", (Proverbs 3:4 NIV). May God give you endurance and encouragement having the same mind one toward another, (Romans 15:5 KJV). "For I know the plans that he has for you, declares the Lord, plans for welfare and not for evil, to give you hope and a future", (Jeremiah 29:11 NLT). May the Lord make your love increase and overflow for each other, (1Thessalonians3:12 NIV). is no love for you like mine.

Printed in the United States
by Baker & Taylor Publisher Services